All Things in Balance

by Tamara Jasmine Burrell

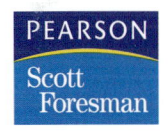

PEARSON
Scott Foresman

Editorial Offices: Glenview, Illinois • Parsippany, New Jersey • New York, New York
Sales Offices: Needham, Massachusetts• Duluth, Georgia • Glenview, Illinois
Coppell, Texas • Sacramento, California • Mesa, Arizona

Herbivores

Thompson's gazelle

grass

Thompson's gazelles are small antelopes. They live with other animals in the grasslands of Africa.

Some scales have two sides. When things weigh the same on both sides, the scale is balanced. One side does not go up, and one side does not go down. Nature has a balance, too. What is the balance of nature?

Let's begin with a few definitions. Some animals eat only plants. They are called herbivores. They are also called plant-eaters or vegetarians. Herbivores graze on leaves and roots, seeds and nuts, fruits and grasses. Some of the biggest herbivores live in Africa. Giraffes, antelopes, zebras, elephants, buffalo, and wildebeests are all herbivores.

---
graze on: eat

Carnivores

cheetah

Thompson's gazelle

Cheetahs eat many kinds of herbivores. They hunt alone or in groups, called packs. One of the most comon foods for cheetahs is the Thompson's gazelle.

Some animals do not eat plants. They eat other animals. They are called carnivores. They are also called meat-eaters or predators. African lions, hyenas, leopards, and cheetahs are all carnivores. The big cats and wolves of North America also are carnivores.

The Thompson's gazelle is one of the cheetah's most common meals. The Thompson's gazelle can run up to 50 miles per hour. A cheetah can run up to 70 mph. But a cheetah can run that fast for only about 300 yards. After 20 seconds the cheetah gets too hot and must stop. The gazelle gets away if it can run faster than the cheetah for more than 20 seconds.

Food Chains

All living things need food. Most plants get their food from water, dirt, and sunshine. Nutrients and decaying matter in the dirt, or soil, feed the plants. Herbivores eat plants. Carnivores eat herbivores or other carnivores. Each living thing provides food for other living things in the food chain.

As you go higher in a food chain, there are fewer kinds of living things. It takes many things at the bottom of a food chain to support the living things at the top.

---

nutrients: substances such as minerals needed to live and grow
decaying matter: dead plants and animals that rot in the soil

Nature in Balance

The balance of nature usually works well. Predators eat some plant-eaters. Some plant-eaters die. Some stay alive. Herbivores eat some of the plants. The plants have enough soil and water. Most of the living things stay healthy.

Nature Out of Balance

Nature depends on balance. So what happens if things get out of balance? If there are too many herbivores, there may not be enough food. The animals get thin. They become scrawny. They may even die of starvation. If the herbivores die, there is less food for predators. Soon, the predators starve and die too.

With no animals to eat them, the plants grow thick. After many years, there are too many plants. The plants fight for water, soil, and sunlight. Eventually, they may get sick and die too.

---

predators: animals that hunt to eat

What Upsets the Balance?

At times, a storm or a flood may upset the balance of nature. Sometimes, humans upset the balance of nature. Sometimes humans help restore it. Here is what happened to one animal: the island fox.

The island fox lives in the Channel Islands of California. This little fox eats insects, birds, eggs, crabs, and small animals such as the deer mouse. It also eats fruit, so it is an omnivore. An omnivore eats both plants and animals.

In the past, this fox had no enemies. Then humans came to the Channel Islands. They brought pigs. Some pigs escaped. Now wild pigs live all over the islands.

Today, the island fox does have an enemy: a predator called the golden eagle. This eagle comes to the islands to eat the wild pigs. It eats foxes too. Now, the island fox is endangered. These little foxes could disappear from our world.

No one wanted to upset the balance of nature in the Channel Islands. People learned that changing one thing can change the balance of an environment. Now people are working there to restore the balance. It takes careful thought and hard work to restore the balance.

Glossary

bal•ance of na•ture
(bal′əns of nā′cher), **NOUN**. a proper balance between plants and animals in one location

car•ni•vore
(kär′nə vôr), **NOUN**. a meat-eating animal; a predator

en•dan•gered
(en dān′jerd) **ADJECTIVE**. in danger of dying out altogether, forever. When all the animals of one kind could die, that kind of animal is called *endangered*.

en•vi•ron•ment
(en vī′rən mənt) **NOUN**. a large area; a place where plants and animals live, eat, and have their young

food chain
(füd chān), **NOUN**. a sequence of organisms in which food passes from one living thing to another. Each living thing is a source of food for others.

her•bi•vore
(ėr′bə vôr), **NOUN**. a plant-eating animal; a vegetarian

om•ni•vore
(om′nə vôr′), **NOUN**. an animal that eats both plants and animals

pred•a•tor
(pred′ə tər), **NOUN**. an animal that lives by hunting and eating other animals

---

Extend Language | **Latin Word Parts**

- The word **carnivore** includes a word part, *carni-*, that comes from the Latin word for "meat."
- The word **herbivore** includes *herbi-*, from a Latin word for certain kinds of plants.
- The word **omnivore** includes *omni-*, from the Latin word for "all."